Little Kitchen

half-hour
HUNGRIES

Little Kitchen

half-hour
HUNGRIES

36 awesome dishes for kids to make
when time is short!

Sabrina Parrini

hardie grant books

MELBOURNE · LONDON

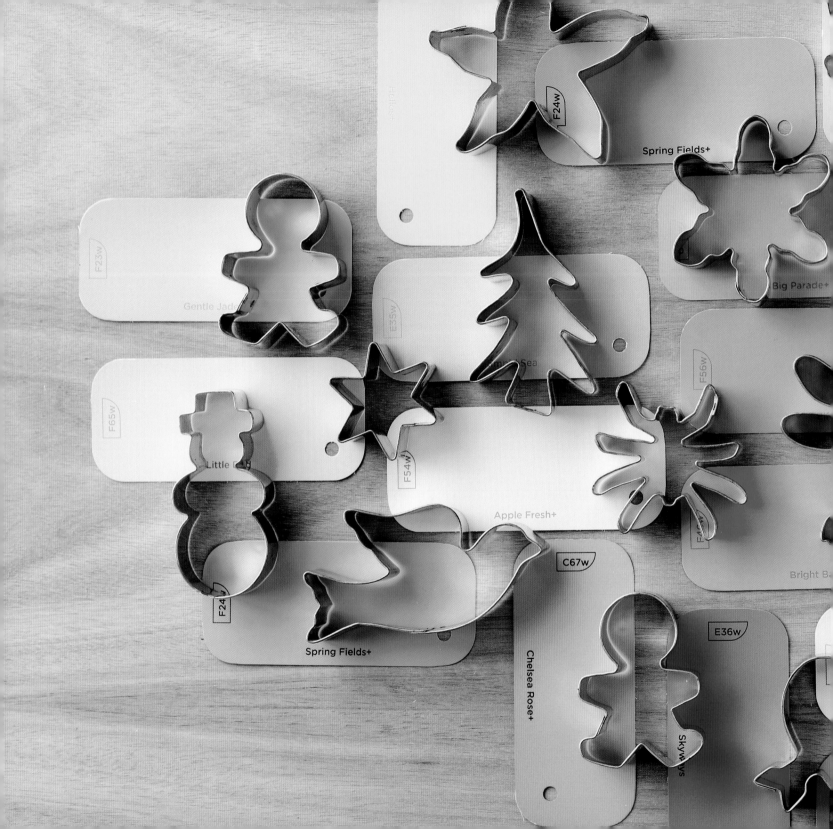

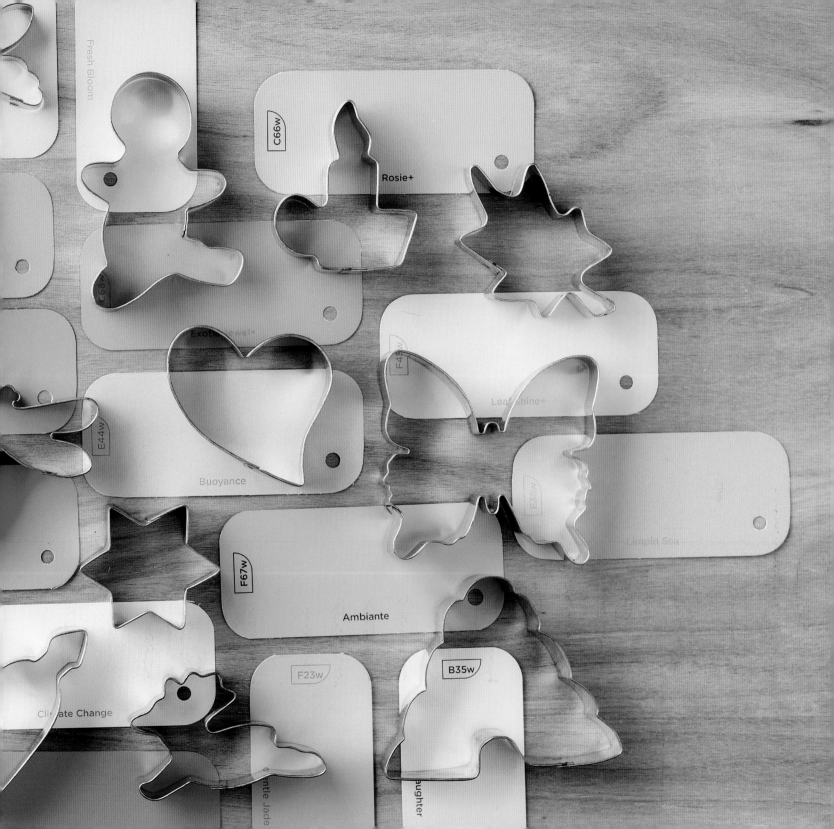

Published in 2013 by Hardie Grant Books

Hardie Grant Books (Australia)
Ground Floor, Building 1
658 Church Street
Richmond, Victoria 3121
www.hardiegrant.com.au

Hardie Grant Books (UK)
Dudley House, North Suite
34–35 Southampton Street
London WC2E 7HF
www.hardiegrant.co.uk

A Cataloguing-in-Publication entry is available from the catalogue
of the National Library of Australia at www.nla.gov.au

Half-hour Hungries
ISBN 978 1 74270 498 2

Publishing Director: Paul McNally
Managing Editor: Lucy Heaver
Editor: Rihana Ries
Design Manager: Heather Menzies
Design Concept: Simone Dutton
Typesetter: Megan Ellis
Photographer: Mark Roper
Stylist: Sabrina Parrini
Home Economist: Caroline Jones
Production Manager: Todd Rechner
Production Assistant: Sarah Trotter

Colour reproduction by Splitting Image Colour Studio
Printed and bound in China by 1010 Printing International Limited

To Chanel, Sisi and Gingerboy.

My babies.

Contents

Dear kids,

Do you often come home hungry after school? Have you ever wanted to cook your family a meal, but don't want to slave away for hours and hours? Are you sick and tired of eating the same old shrink-wrapped snacks every day?

Then this is the book for you!

I like cooking and I love eating, but sometimes I just feel like whipping up a fast and tasty treat. I know you've got school to go to, homework to do and friends to hang out with. So I've made sure that *Half-hour Hungries* is full of awesome recipes you can cook in roughly 30 minutes, to leave time for other important things in your life.

So grab your apron, pick up your mixing spoon and let's get cracking!

Lots of love,

Sabrina x

Dear parents,

Thanks for buying this book!

I learnt to cook when I was really young. When I was eight years old, I bought my first-ever cookbook, *Cool and Creamy: The Ice-cream and Frozen Yoghurt Book*, at a school fete. It was love at first sight – I spent months poring over each page. I even went so far as to colour in all of the black-and-white recipe illustrations!

This book still sits on my bookshelf, decades later. I look at it from time to time and good memories come flowing back: memories of after-school cooking adventures and lazy Sundays spent experimenting with different ice cream flavours and toppings.

I remember my mum's country-style kitchen, with its daggy brown tiles and olive green bench. I remember being impatient waiting for my ice cream to set, and proud when I could finally serve it to my family.

I don't know if what I cooked was any good, but I remember my mum encouraging me nonetheless. Back then, my kitchen may not have been filled with culinary greatness, but I recall the time I spent cooking there with great fondness. I hope this book will help your child create similar happy memories in the kitchen.

So here's to our children, their enthusiasm and every culinary masterpiece they create.

Lots of love,

Sabrina x

How to use this book

30 minutes? Too easy!

Thanks to the efforts of my 25 little recipe testers, I found that most of the dishes in this book can be cooked in roughly 30 minutes.

This is an estimate, though – the timing also depends on how old and experienced in the kitchen you are. You'll get quicker and more confident the more you practise – so keep cooking!

When I first thought about writing this book, I knew it'd be dangerous to get you to rush around collecting the ingredients, assembling the equipment, prepping the food and cooking the recipe in 30 minutes. So for now, to be safe, just try to do the cooking part of the recipe – from the method onwards – and see how you go with the 30-minute time frame.

Don't rush, though! Unlike a *MasterChef* challenge, cooking from this book isn't a race.

This book is split into three chapters:

- Speedy Snacks – recipes that can be cooked in 10–20 minutes
- Easy Eats – recipes that can be cooked in 20–30 minutes
- Bigger Bites – recipes that can be cooked in 30 minutes or more

Every recipe has a rough timing guide to help you plan your meal. Prep time refers to the time it takes to collect your ingredients and equipment, and prepare everything as directed in the ingredient list. Cooking time refers to the time it takes to follow the actual method section of the recipe.

Although cooking is great fun, it's important to remember that some things in the kitchen can be dangerous if you're not careful. For this reason, it's very important to have an adult stay in the kitchen with you the whole time you're cooking.

Knives and sharp equipment

Knives, peelers, graters and food processors are sharp, so when they are called for in a recipe, I recommend that an adult should always be close by to help. Very small children may not be experienced or big enough to use knives safely, in which case an adult should do what is required.

Sharp knives are safer than blunt knives because you don't need to use as much pressure to cut with them. When you use less pressure, you are less likely to slip and cut yourself.

Don't put a knife – or anything sharp – into a sink of water for washing where it can't be seen. If someone doesn't know it's there, they might cut themselves.

Oven and stovetop

Ovens and stovetops get very hot, so I recommend that an adult should always be present when they are in use. Ask an adult to help you turn the heat on and off and to adjust the temperature to the correct level.

When using the oven, remember to place your oven trays on the right shelves BEFORE you turn it on. In general, the middle shelf is the best spot for cooking, because it allows the hot air to move all around your dish and cook the food evenly.

Stand back when the oven door is being opened as the hot steam can burn. Both adults and children should use oven mitts when moving things in and out of the oven. Ideally, they should be long enough to cover your forearms – and please make sure they are the right size for your hands: small mitts for small hands.

When cooking on the stovetop, always ask an adult to turn the heat on and to adjust it to the correct temperature. Either you or an adult MUST hold the handle steady when stirring something in a pan on the stovetop. Always wear oven mitts when working near a stovetop or with hot ingredients.

Turn the handles of pots and pans so they face to the back or side of the stove. Handles poking out could cause an accident if someone accidentally knocks them. Never leave them unattended and always remember to turn the heat off when you're finished.

Always use a timer, so you don't overcook or burn anything; it's easy to forget how long something has been cooking! Never leave the kitchen when you have something on the stovetop as it may burn or catch on fire.

Spills

Always clean up spills straight away. Spills on the floor make it slippery and you could slip and fall over. Wipe up with paper towels and once you've cleaned up, tell everyone else to be careful of the wet floor.

Allergies

If you don't already know, check with your parents or an adult to find out if you're allergic to any foods. If you are, ALWAYS tell the adult you are cooking with before you start. They might not know or they might have forgotten. Make sure you both check the recipe carefully to make sure it doesn't use any ingredients you can't have. If you're unsure about something, it's safer to choose another recipe instead.

Food safety

It's important to follow some simple hygiene rules when cooking so that no one gets sick! If you're cooking with both raw meats and vegetables, make sure you use two separate chopping boards and never use the same knife to chop vegetables after you've cut up meat. This is because raw meats sometimes have bacteria in them (that are killed by the cooking process), and you don't want them to end up on your veggies!

Ingredients

Although *Half-hour Hungries* focuses on quick, healthy and wholesome food, we also believe that eating is about balance. That means we do sometimes use sugar, butter, cream and cheese in our recipes. You could say we're into being healthy, but without taking it to extremes.

Unless I specify something else in the recipe, these are the ingredients I recommend you use:

- Onions are brown onions.

- All garlic cloves are peeled.

- Milk is full-cream.

- Cream is full-fat (low-fat cream does not whip).

- Meat is free-range and lean.

- Canned tuna is preserved in oil and without added flavourings.

- Eggs are 60 gram, free-range, and should be brought to room temperature before cooking.

- Quality brands of pasta and risotto rice are less likely to break apart during the cooking process than the cheapest brands.

- You can use either vanilla-bean paste or vanilla extract in the recipes.

- Stock is homemade if possible as the flavour is so much nicer.

Equipment

For each recipe you'll find a list of the equipment that you'll need to prepare the dish.

Knives and chopping boards

Use a bigger knife for bigger ingredients and a smaller knife for small ingredients. Serrated knives are best for slicing bread. Remember that all knives should be kept sharp, as blunt knives are more dangerous.

Always use a chopping board when you're using a knife so that you don't scratch the kitchen bench or tabletop. It is important that the board doesn't slip around on the bench, so either use one that has a non-slip rubber base or rubber feet, or place a damp tea towel beneath the board to keep it steady. A bigger board is better, as you have more room to work on.

Use two chopping boards if you need to prepare meat and vegetables in the same recipe.

Scissors

Scissors are ideal for snipping herbs. Use small, child-safe scissors where possible.

Graters and peelers

Little chefs will find a box grater is easiest for grating and zesting. Conical graters and microplane graters may be suitable for older children, but they do require a little more dexterity because of their shape and the angle at which you need to hold the food. Try to use a grater that has a rubber handle on it and a non-slip rubber base to prevent accidents occurring due to loss of steadiness.

It takes a bit of practice to use a peeler. Try to hold food steady on a chopping board and peel in long smooth movements, rather than little bits at a time.

Measuring jugs, measuring cups, measuring spoons

Although sometimes you will have to weigh an ingredient out using kitchen scales, wherever possible, I've suggested using measuring jugs, cups and spoons to measure ingredients.

Don't use regular cups and spoons because they come in all sorts of different shapes and sizes, which means they won't be accurate.

This book uses standard Australian metric measures (1 tablespoon = 20 ml, 1 cup = 250 ml). American and European measures are a little bit different (1 tablespoon = 15 ml, 1 cup = 240 ml or 285 ml), so check your measuring equipment carefully to see which it is.

Jugs are for measuring liquids, like milk and stock. To measure accurately, sit the jug on the work surface and measure the ingredient to the marked line – not over or under it.

Cups are for measuring solid ingredients, like rice or flour. To measure accurately, heap the ingredient up high, then use a spatula to smooth over the top and make it level.

Spoons are for measuring smaller amounts of liquids or solids, such as honey or milk, baking powder or sugar. To measure accurately, heap the ingredient up high, then use a spatula to smooth over the top to make it level.

Mixing bowls

I recommend you have several different-sized mixing bowls – small, medium and large – to match the quantity of ingredients. Metal or plastic bowls are ideal as they are light and won't break if you drop them. Shallow bowls make mixing easier for children. When mixing in a bowl, use one hand to hold it steady on the work surface and one hand to mix.

Food processors and electric mixers

Both these machines make kitchen work easier! Food processors are great for chopping ingredients quickly or turning them into a paste. Sometimes you have to scrape the ingredients down from the sides of the bowl so they mix in properly. Always make sure an adult puts in and removes the sharp blade and that they help you turn the machine on and off.

Electric mixers make baking cakes and biscuits (cookies) easy. An adult should help you fit the correct attachment to the machine, help you set the correct speed and watch while you use it. A paddle attachment is used for beating, while a whisk is used to whip cream or egg whites.

Saucepans

I use a set of different-sized saucepans with a spout for easy pouring. Smaller saucepans are perfect for melting butter or chocolate or cooking smaller quantities. Use a large saucepan for cooking soup, pasta or rice. Saucepans should have a tight-fitting lid and a handle that won't get hot when you are cooking.

Frying pans

As the name suggests, these are for frying ingredients – often in a little bit of oil or butter. Non-stick pans are great because you can fry without oil and they are very easy to clean. Use a deeper pan for deep-frying. Some ingredients, such as nuts and spices, are dry-roasted without oil. Make sure your frying pans have a handle that won't get hot when you are cooking.

Colanders

These are used to drain boiled vegetables and pasta. Always ask an adult to help you and be careful to stand away from the hot steam. The safest way to drain hot items is to place the colander in the sink and pour the hot contents in.

Sieves and sifters

These have a fine mesh and are used to sift flour, icing sugar or cocoa to remove any lumps. They are often used when making cakes or batters, to ensure the mixture is smooth and light.

Oven

We used a fan-forced oven to test the recipes in this book. Generally, fan-forced ovens cook faster than other ovens, so you might need to adjust cooking temperatures and times if you have a conventional oven.

Equipment

Baking trays, cake tins and muffin tins

Baking trays are metal trays for cooking things in the oven. Some are deep and are used for roasting meat. Shallow baking trays are used for cooking things like biscuits. Often, baking trays will need to be greased before use to stop food sticking. Use a piece of scrunched-up baking paper to rub the tray all over with a little butter or oil.

Cake tins and muffin tins come in different shapes and sizes. Make sure you use the correct size for the recipe you are preparing and grease or line it with baking paper according to the instructions.

Baking dishes and ovenproof dishes

These are dishes that can be used in the oven without breaking. They are used for bakes, slices, casseroles and pies.

Wire racks

These are essential for cooling cakes or biscuits after they come out of the oven.

Utensils

Spoons can be wooden or metal and are used for stirring. In general, I recommend using spoons with long handles when stirring something in a pan on the stovetop to keep hands well away from hot contents. Slotted spoons are useful for lifting solid ingredients, such as gnocchi, out of a liquid.

Tongs are perfect for moving things around in a pan or on the barbecue.

Whisks are used when you want to remove lumps to make a smooth sauce, or when you want to incorporate some air into ingredients such as cream or egg whites.

Bowl scrapers and **palette knives** are perfect for scraping out bowls or for spreading fillings or icings onto cakes.

Spatulas are useful for turning all sorts of things over in pans or for lifting them out.

Ladles are perfect for serving soups and stews as they hold more than spoons.

Biscuit (cookie) cutters come in all sorts of fun shapes and sizes and are great for making biscuits or scones.

Pastry brushes are used to brush pastry with melted butter, egg or milk before baking, so that it turns golden and shiny. A brush can also be used to marinate meat before cooking.

Plastic wrap comes in rolls and is used to wrap and seal food to stop it from drying out in the air.

Kitchen towel is absorbent paper that is used for mopping up spills in the kitchen or for draining food that has been fried.

Baking paper is often lightly coated in silicon and is used to line baking trays and cake tins so that biscuits or cakes won't stick.

Time-saving tips

Rushing around in the kitchen is never a good idea: it can cause you to make mistakes, or worse, hurt yourself. There are safe ways to speed up the cooking process without putting your health at risk, though – here are a few suggestions.

- Put your apron on and tie your hair back if it's long.
- Read the whole recipe through first before you start cooking. Make sure you understand everything. If you don't, ask an adult to explain.
- Follow the time-saving tips for each recipe.
- Have all of the ingredients and equipment neatly laid out on your work surface.
- Find an adult to be your kitchen hand. Ask them (nicely!) to help you with ingredient preparation.
- Measure out all of the ingredients into the correct amounts.
- Use a food processor to finely dice onion and garlic. You can also use it to grate cheese and veggies with the grater attachment.
- Pre-heat your oven and boil and salt pasta water in advance, if necessary.
- Have a garbage bin nearby to keep the kitchen tidy.
- Clean as you go. No one likes a messy cook, or a messy kitchen!
- Before you cook, make sure you have a clean, uncluttered work surface.
- Set your table beforehand, so when the food is ready you can tuck in!

Speedy Snacks

Recipes you can cook
in 10–20 minutes

Summer sunset juice

This juice is not just pretty to look at – it tastes amazing and is packed with vitamins, too! This recipe calls for grenadine, which is a sweet, red syrup made from pomegranate.

Serves 2
Prep time: 30 minutes
Cooking time: 20 minutes

Ingredients

300 g (10½ oz) watermelon, rind removed, diced roughly

5 oranges, peeled and quartered

15 g (½ oz/¼ cup firmly packed) mint leaves

5 large ice cubes

1 tablespoon grenadine

2 sprigs mint, to garnish

Time-saving tips

Have all your equipment and ingredients ready

Find a kitchen hand to help you prepare the ingredients ahead of time

Method

Position the jug of your juicer underneath the juicer spout.

Switch the juicer on and carefully feed in the watermelon, orange quarters and mint leaves. If your juicer's jug is too small to hold all of the juice in one go, feed in the fruit in batches and transfer the juice into a larger jug.

Using a spoon, skim off and throw away any foam sitting on top of the juice. Add the ice to the jug and mix well. Divide the juice between 2 tall glasses, using a spoon to prevent the ice from falling in.

Measure the grenadine into a small glass. Use a drinking straw to suck up half of the grenadine – try not to drink any! With two fingers, tightly pinch the top of the straw and place the straw into the bottom of one glass of juice. Relax your grip on the straw – this will release the grenadine at the bottom of the glass. Repeat this process for the second glass of juice.

The grenadine is heavier than the fruit juice, so it will sit at the bottom of the glass while the fruit juice floats on top!

Garnish with the sprigs of mint and serve immediately with a straw in each glass. Mix well before drinking.

Equipment:

Chopping board

Sharp knife

Scales

Measuring spoons

Juicer with jug

Metal tablespoon

2 tall drinking glasses

Small glass

3 drinking straws

Mango smoothie

My husband, Anthony, taught me how to make this amazing drink a few years ago. Now I make it every time we have a big party. I hope you love it as much as I do!

Serves 2
Prep time: 10 minutes
Cooking time: 10 minutes

Ingredients

2 large mango cheeks, peeled and frozen
1 egg white
1 tablespoon sugar syrup
400 ml (13½ fl oz/1⅗ cups) milk

Time-saving tips

Have all your equipment and ingredients ready

Find a kitchen hand to help you prepare the ingredients ahead of time

Skin and freeze several mango cheeks in advance, so you have them on hand

Use ready-made sugar syrup

Method

Put mango cheeks, egg white, sugar syrup and milk into the jug of your blender.

With the lid on, blend on high for a minute, or until all of the mango has been puréed.

Carefully pour the smoothie into 2 glasses and serve immediately.

Equipment:

Measuring spoons

Measuring jug

Blender

2 tall drinking glasses

Nacho-flavoured popcorn

This is a tasty variation on buttered popcorn that one of my Little Kitchen teachers, Lisa, taught my cooking students. Serve it at your next party or for National Popcorn Day – 19 January. It's sure to be a hit!

Makes approximately 5 cups

Prep time: 15 minutes

Cooking time: 15-20 minutes

Ingredients

2 tablespoons vegetable oil

70 g (2½ oz/⅓ cup) popping corn

30 g (1 oz/1½ tablespoons) salted butter

½ teaspoon sweet paprika

½ teaspoon garlic powder

½ teaspoon onion powder

½ teaspoon sea salt

30 g (1 oz/⅓ cup) parmesan cheese,
   finely grated

Time-saving tips

Have all your equipment and ingredients ready

Find a kitchen hand to help you prepare the ingredients ahead of time

Method

Measure the oil into a large, heavy-based saucepan and add two kernels of popping corn.

With adult help: Heat the saucepan over medium–high heat. When the two kernels pop, tip the remaining popping corn into the saucepan and quickly put the lid on. Wearing an oven mitt, hold the lid on tight and gently swirl the pan around so all of the popping corn gets coated in oil.

Soon you'll hear the corn start to pop! Keep the lid on and don't peek, because the corn could escape from the pan and burn you. If you really want to see what's happening, try using a saucepan with a glass lid.

With adult help: Give the pan a gentle shake with the lid on while the corn is popping. After roughly a minute, when the sound of popping has slowed to 1 or 2 pops every 5 seconds, take the saucepan off the heat. Leave the lid on until the corn has stopped popping completely.

With adult help: Wearing oven mitts, use a large measuring cup to scoop the popcorn into a bowl. Leave any dark bits in the bottom of the pan. These are the corn kernels that didn't pop or open all the way and may have burnt – there are usually a few in every batch.

With adult help: In a small saucepan, melt the butter over medium heat. Once the butter has melted, remove the pan from the heat and add the spices and salt. Mix well, then evenly pour the butter mixture over the popcorn. Using a metal spoon, stir well. Add the grated parmesan and quickly combine so the cheese sticks to the popcorn. Serve immediately.

Equipment:

 Measuring cups

 Scales

 Chopping board

 Sharp knife

 Grater

 Measuring spoons

 Large, heavy-based saucepan with lid

 Oven mitts

 Small saucepan

 Large bowl · Large metal, kitchen spoon

Salsa fresca with corn chips

This refreshing summer snack was inspired by a salsa I enjoyed at a Mexican restaurant many years ago. It's best eaten within a few hours of being made. *Fresca* means 'fresh' in Spanish!

Serves 2

Prep time: 20 minutes

Cooking time: 15 minutes

Ingredients

3 ripe medium tomatoes, cut into 1 cm
  (½ inch) cubes
1 teaspoon firmly packed coriander
  (cilantro) leaves
1 teaspoon fresh lime juice
½ teaspoon ground coriander
½ teaspoon ground cumin
1 teaspoon sea salt
Corn (tortilla) chips, to serve

Time-saving tips

Have all your equipment and ingredients ready

Find a kitchen hand to help you prepare the ingredients ahead of time

Method

Place the chopped tomatoes in a non-reactive mixing bowl.

Using your fingers, tear up the coriander leaves and add them to the bowl.

Pour in the lime juice and add the ground coriander, cumin and sea salt.

Mix well using a metal spoon. Refrigerate for at least 10 minutes before serving, so the flavours soak into the tomatoes.

Check for seasoning before serving alongside a bowl of corn chips.

Equipment:

 Chopping board

 Sharp knife

 Measuring spoons

 Medium non-reactive mixing bowl

 Juicer

 Metal kitchen spoon

corn chips

lime

salsa
fresca

Garlic green beans with parmesan and almonds

This is a recipe for those of you who enjoy fancy food or, as I like to call it, 'posh nosh'. It's a simple but tasty side dish that is a favourite on many restaurant menus!

Serves 4 as a side dish

Prep time: 30 minutes

Cooking time: 15 minutes

Ingredients

200 g (7 oz) green beans, trimmed
2 tablespoons flaked almonds
20 g (1 oz/1 tablespoon) salted butter
2 small garlic cloves, finely grated
  or crushed
20 g (1 oz) parmesan cheese

Time-saving tips

Have all your equipment and ingredients ready

Find a kitchen hand to help you prepare the ingredients ahead of time

Method

With adult help: Boil your kettle and use it to fill a saucepan one-quarter of the way up. Place the steamer basket in the saucepan and fill with the beans, ensuring that the water doesn't touch the bottom of the steamer. Steam the beans over medium heat until the beans are tender, but still green. Once cooked, remove from heat and set aside.

With adult help: Meanwhile, heat a frying pan over low heat. Add the almonds and toast, stirring regularly with a wooden spoon, for around 3 minutes, or until golden brown and lightly toasted. Remove the almonds from the pan so they don't keep cooking and set aside. In the same frying pan, melt the butter over low heat. Add the garlic and cook for 1 minute, stirring well – make sure you don't let it burn, as burnt garlic tastes yuck!

With adult help: Place the cooked beans in a mixing bowl. Pour over the garlic butter mixture and, using a wooden spoon, stir to coat well. Add the toasted almonds and mix through gently.

Using tongs, arrange the beans on a serving platter. Drizzle with the leftover garlic butter mixture. Shave the parmesan using a speed peeler, then sprinkle over the beans. Serve immediately.

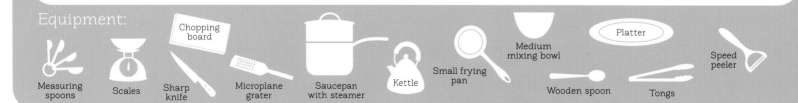

Equipment: Measuring spoons · Scales · Chopping board · Sharp knife · Microplane grater · Saucepan with steamer · Kettle · Small frying pan · Medium mixing bowl · Platter · Wooden spoon · Tongs · Speed peeler

parmesan
cheese

green
beans

toasted
almonds

Cadbury's
CHOCOLATES
Waratah

HALF C...
JER...
MA...
VANI...
ICE CR...

JERSEY MAID ICE CREAM COMP...

Peters

THE HEALTH FOOD OF A NATION

VANILLA
ICE CREAM
FOUR LITRES

Peters ICE CREAM PTY. LTD. S.A. F22
ARTIFICIALLY COLOURED & FLAVOURED

Roses
Chocolates

White Heather

Pascall

chocolates and toffees

Hibiscus
CHOCOLATE & TOFFEE
ASSORTMENT

Made by
MacRobertson

Savoury French toast

My aunty Lella taught me how to make savoury French toast when I was younger. I was used to my mum's sweet version, and remember being surprised by how delicious savoury French toast was. This is great served with roasted tomatoes!

Makes 2 large pieces of French toast

Prep time: 10 minutes

Cooking time: 20 minutes

Ingredients

1 egg
60 ml (2 fl oz/¼ cup) milk
½ teaspoon sea salt
1 pinch finely ground black pepper
1 tablespoon vegetable oil, for frying
2 slices of casalinga or sourdough bread,
 about 1.5 cm (½ in) thick, cut on
 the diagonal

Time-saving tips

Have all your equipment and ingredients ready

Find a kitchen hand to help you prepare the ingredients ahead of time

Method

Crack the egg into a mixing bowl. Add the milk, salt and pepper and whisk until frothy.

Measure the oil into a frying pan.

Take one slice of bread and place it in the egg mixture for roughly 30 seconds. Flip the bread over and let it sit in the egg mixture until soaked through – roughly another 30 seconds.

With adult help: While the bread soaks, heat the frying pan over medium–low heat for 30 seconds.

With adult help: Carefully place the eggy bread into the heated pan – watch for splashing! While this first piece cooks, repeat the soaking process with the remaining slice of bread and add it to the pan when it is soaked through.

With adult help: After 2 minutes cooking time, turn the first piece of French toast over with a spatula. A minute later, turn the second piece of French toast. Once flipped, each piece of French toast should be cooked for a further 2 minutes, or until golden.

With adult help: Using a spatula, carefully remove the French toast from the pan and place on the absorbent paper-covered plate to soak up any excess oil. Serve immediately.

Equipment:

Large mixing bowl

Measuring jug

Measuring spoons

Whisk

Spatula

Frying pan

Large plate covered in kitchen towel

Super-speedy margherita pizza

This recipe is the Speedy Gonzales of pizzas, because you don't need to make your own pizza dough and wait ages for it to rise! Choose any toppings you like – I've chosen margherita, as it's a true Italian classic.

Makes 2 pizzas
Prep time: 25 minutes
Cooking time: 15 minutes

Ingredients

2 mini pita breads
60 g (2 oz/¼ cup) tomato paste
1 medium garlic clove, finely grated
  or crushed
2 tablespoons olive oil
1 teaspoon salt
1 pinch finely ground black pepper
80 g (3 oz) mozzarella cheese, grated
1 tablespoon firmly packed basil leaves

Method

Preheat your oven to 180ºC (350ºF). Place the pita breads on a baking tray and set aside.

In a non-reactive mixing bowl, combine the tomato paste, garlic, olive oil, salt and pepper. Using a small palette knife, evenly divide and spread the tomato paste mixture on both pita breads. Top each with a sprinkling of cheese and then scatter over the basil leaves.

With adult help: Wearing oven mitts, place the baking tray on the middle shelf of the oven. Cook the pizzas for roughly 10 minutes, or until the cheese is melted and golden. Once again wearing oven mitts, remove the baking tray from the oven.

Using a spatula, carefully transfer the pizzas to a serving platter. Using a pizza cutter (or, with adult help, a sharp knife), slice the pizzas into quarters. Serve immediately.

Time-saving tips

Have all your equipment and ingredients ready

Find a kitchen hand to help you prepare the ingredients ahead of time

Pre-heat your oven to 180ºC (350ºF) at least 20 minutes before cooking

Have an oven tray positioned in the middle shelf of the oven

Equipment:

Measuring spoons · Scales · Grater · Sharp knife · Chopping board · Baking tray · Medium non-reactive mixing bowl · Spatula · Kitchen spoon · Oven mitts · Platter · Pizza cutter · Small palette knife or bowl scraper

ALL THE TOOLS YOU NEED TO MAK

Rocket and pear salad

This refreshing salad is a classic dish! Make this just before you need to eat it, because the pear oxidises, or goes brown, very quickly once you've cut it.

Serves 4–6 as a side dish

Prep time: 30 minutes

Cooking time: 20 minutes

Ingredients

Salad dressing
60 ml (2 fl oz/¼ cup) lemon juice
   (from roughly 1 medium lemon)
60 ml (2 fl oz/¼ cup) vegetable oil
2 heaped teaspoons soft brown sugar
1 teaspoon dijon mustard

Salad
1 just-ripe brown pear, quartered and
   thinly sliced
100 g (3½ oz/2½ cups firmly packed)
   rocket (arugula) leaves
50 g (2 oz/1½ cups) watercress leaves
50 g (2 oz/½ cup) candied walnuts
   (see Note)
50 g (2 oz) parmesan cheese

Method

To make the dressing, put all of the dressing ingredients into a screw-top jar. Tighten the lid and vigorously shake until well combined, about a minute. Set aside.

Using clean hands, gently combine the pear, rocket, watercress and walnuts in a large non-reactive mixing bowl.

Pour 2 tablespoons of dressing over the salad and gently toss with your hands before transferring to a serving platter. The remaining dressing will keep in the refrigerator for up to a week.

Wash your hands, then shave the parmesan over the salad using a speed peeler. Don't mix it through, as it will get soggy! Serve immediately.

Note
Candied walnuts can be found in gourmet food stores and some supermarkets.

Time-saving tips
Have all your equipment and ingredients ready

Find a kitchen hand to help you prepare the ingredients ahead of time

Equipment:

 Measuring jug

 Measuring spoons

 Sharp knife

Chopping board

 Scales

 Juicer

 Medium screw-top jar

 Large non-reactive mixing bowl

 Speed peeler

Serving platter

crisp pear

caramelised
walnut

parmesan
cheese

Vanilla yoghurt with watermelon and rosewater

Refreshing, impressive and simple to prepare! Rachel, one of the amazing cooking teachers at Little Kitchen, taught me this.

Serves 4

Prep time: 20 minutes

Cooking time: 15 minutes

Ingredients

250 g (9 oz/1 cup) thick, sweetened Greek-style yoghurt

1 tablespoon caster (superfine) sugar

1½ teaspoons natural vanilla extract

3 tablespoons unsalted pistachios

500 g (1 lb 2 oz) seedless watermelon, cut into 2 cm (¾ in) cubes

1½ tablespoons rosewater

8 perfect mint leaves

4 tufts of pistachio-flavoured Persian fairy floss (see Note)

Time-saving tips

Have all your equipment and ingredients ready

Find a kitchen hand to help you prepare the ingredients ahead of time

Method

Spoon the yoghurt into a mixing bowl. Combine well with the caster sugar and vanilla. Set aside.

Using a food processor, chop half of the pistachios for about 40 seconds.

With adult help: Turn the processor off at the power outlet and remove the processor blade. Combine the chopped pistachios with the remaining whole pistachios and set aside.

Evenly divide the watermelon cubes between four serving bowls. Sprinkle half a teaspoon of rosewater over each bowl. Then, using a tablespoon, evenly dollop on the vanilla yoghurt mixture.

Garnish with the chopped and whole pistachios, a few mint leaves and a tuft of Persian fairy floss. Serve immediately.

Note

Persian fairy floss can be found in Middle Eastern supermarkets and some gourmet food stores.

Equipment:

Measuring spoons

Scales

Sharp knife

Chopping board

Medium mixing bowl

Metal tablespoon

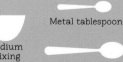

Large metal kitchen spoon

Food processor

4 small serving bowls

Persian
fairy floss

pistachio

watermelon

Knickerbocker glory

This is my take on a kind of fancy ice cream sundae from the United Kingdom. If you like, you can also layer in orange, raspberry or strawberry jelly!

Serves 4

Prep time: 20 minutes

Cooking time: 10-15 minutes

Ingredients

1 large jam Swiss roll (jelly roll)
250 ml (8½ fl oz/1 cup) quality
    ready-made pouring custard
16 tinned peach slices, drained
8 scoops vanilla-bean ice cream
125 g (4½ oz/1 cup) raspberries
300 ml (10½ fl oz/1¼ cup)
    softly whipped cream
4 red glacé cherries
20 g (¾ oz) crushed peanuts
4 Scandinavian-style ginger thins
    (see Note)

Method

With adult help: Cut the Swiss roll into 8 and divide the slices between 4 tall dessert glasses. Press the Swiss roll slices firmly into the bottom, then pour 60 ml (2 fl oz/¼ cup) of the custard into each glass.

Add 4 peach quarters, followed by a scoop of vanilla ice cream, to each glass. If you put your ice cream scoop in a bowl of boiling water, it makes scooping the ice cream easier.

Divide the raspberries between the four glasses, then evenly dollop the cream on top. Garnish each with a glacé cherry and the crushed peanuts. Finish with a ginger thin and serve immediately with a sundae spoon.

Note

Scandinavian-style ginger thins, or *pepparkakor*, can be found in the international food section of some supermarkets and in some gourmet food stores. You can substitute them with any thin ginger biscuit (cookie).

Time-saving tips

Have all your equipment and ingredients ready

Find a kitchen hand to help you prepare the ingredients ahead of time

Equipment:

 Measuring jug

 Scales

 Chopping board / Sharp knife

 Can opener / Ice cream scoop

 Medium bowl (filled with boiling water)

 Metal kitchen spoon

 Electric mixer

 4 tall dessert glasses

 4 sundae spoons

ginger
biscuit

raspberries

peach

Swiss roll

Easy Eats

Recipes you can cook
in 20-30 minutes

Cheesy quesadillas

Quesadillas are a great snack food – kind of like a Mexican toasted cheese sandwich. In fact, *queso* is what they call cheese in Mexico!

Serves 2 as a snack

Prep time: 20 minutes

Cooking time: 20 minutes

Ingredients

2 x 20 cm (8 in) flour tortillas
100 g (3½ oz) cheddar cheese, grated
1 medium tomato, chopped into
    1 cm (½ in) cubes
1 spring onion (scallion), finely sliced
50 g (1¾ oz/¼ cup) corn kernels (fresh
    or canned)
2 teaspoons coriander (cilantro) leaves,
    finely chopped, plus extra to garnish
Sour cream or guacamole, to serve

Method

Place 1 tortilla on a chopping board and set the other aside.

In a mixing bowl, combine the cheese, tomato, spring onion, corn and 2 teaspoons of coriander. Evenly spread the cheese mixture onto the tortilla on the chopping board. Place the other tortilla on top and press down lightly.

With adult help: Turn on your sandwich press and let it heat up. When hot, carefully place the quesadilla in and press shut. Cook the quesadilla until the cheese has completely melted and the tortillas are lightly golden. Using a spatula, slide the quesadilla onto a platter.

Using a pizza cutter (or, with adult help, a sharp knife), cut the quesadilla into 6–8 wedges. Garnish with coriander and serve immediately with sour cream or guacamole.

Note

If you don't have a sandwich press at home, ask an adult to help you heat a frying pan over low heat, then slide the quesadilla into the pan using a spatula. Cook for two minutes on each side, then use a spatula to transfer the quesadilla to a plate.

Time-saving tips

Have all your equipment and ingredients ready

Find a kitchen hand to help you prepare the ingredients ahead of time

Use pre-grated cheese

Equipment:

Measuring spoons | Scales | Chopping board | Sharp knife | Metal kitchen spoon | Can opener | Grater | Mixing bowl | Large, wide spatula | Sandwich press | Platter | Pizza cutter

toasted
tortilla

cheesy
filling

Cheese twists

These tasty treats make great party food! If you prefer, you can cut them in half to create 24 small twists.

Makes 12 large or 24 small twists

Prep time: 20 minutes

Cooking time: 20–30 minutes

Ingredients

1 tablespoon plain (all-purpose) flour
2 x 24 cm (9½ in) squares ready-made
  puff pastry, thawed
60 ml (2 fl oz/¼ cup) tomato sauce
  (ketchup)
100 g (3½ oz) cheddar cheese, grated

Time-saving tips

Have all your equipment and ingredients ready

Find a kitchen hand to help you prepare the ingredients ahead of time

Pre-heat your oven to 190°C (375°F) at least 20 minutes before cooking

Method

Pre-heat your oven to 190° C (375°F). Line a baking tray with baking paper and dust your chopping board with the flour.

Gently pull the plastic backing sheet off one pastry square and place it on the chopping board. Pour the tomato sauce into the centre of this pastry square. Using a small bowl scraper, evenly spread the sauce over the pastry. Top with an even sprinkling of the cheese.

Carefully place the other pastry square on top so the whole thing resembles a cheese and sauce sandwich. Using clean hands, gently but firmly press down all over the pastry to seal the two squares together. Gently pull the plastic backing sheet off the second pastry square.

With adult help: Using a sharp knife, slice the pastry from top to bottom to make roughly twelve 2 cm (¾ in) wide strips. You can use a ruler for this step, if you like.

With adult help: Hold one end of a pastry strip and ask an adult to hold the other end. Turn the pastry in opposite directions until the pastry is completely twisted, taking care that no filling falls out. Place the twist on the baking tray and repeat until all the strips are twisted. Remove any loose bits of cheese from the tray before you place it in the oven.

With adult help: Wearing oven mitts, place the baking tray in the oven and cook for about 20 minutes, or until the pastry is puffed and golden. Once more wearing oven mitts, remove the cooked twists from the oven and cool for 3 minutes.

Using a spatula, transfer the cheese twists to a serving platter. These are best eaten warm!

Equipment: Measuring jug, Measuring spoons, Sharp knife, Chopping board, Scales, Grater, Baking paper, Large non-stick baking tray, Ruler, Small bowl scraper, Spatula, Oven mitts, Platter

Corn muffins

These are a true American classic! I've amped up the flavour by adding cheese and paprika.

Makes 12

Prep time: 20 minutes

Cooking time: 20 minutes

Ingredients

2 eggs
250 ml (8½ fl oz/1 cup) milk
100 g (3½ oz) salted butter, melted
90 g (3 oz/¼ cup) honey
¼ teaspoon sweet paprika
¼ teaspoon hot paprika
1 teaspoon sea salt
150 g (5½ oz/1 cup) instant polenta (cornmeal)
100 g (3½ oz) parmesan cheese, finely grated
6 chives
150 g (5½ oz/1 cup) self-raising flour

Method

Pre-heat your oven to 180°C (350°F). Line a muffin tin with paper cases and set aside.

Whisk the eggs, milk, butter, honey, sweet and hot paprika, and salt in a mixing bowl until well combined. Add the polenta and cheese, then carefully use scissors to finely snip in the chives. Stir well. Sift in the self-raising flour and stir until just combined – don't worry if the mixture is lumpy.

Using a tablespoon, fill the paper cases with muffin mixture until three-quarters full.

With adult help: Wearing oven mitts, place the muffin tin on the middle shelf of the oven. Cook the muffins for 20 minutes, or until a metal skewer inserted in the middle of a muffin comes out clean. Once again wearing oven mitts, remove the muffin tin from the oven.

Allow to cool for a few minutes, until you can handle the muffins comfortably. Serve with a smear of butter or dipped into a hearty soup.

Time-saving tips

Have all your equipment and ingredients ready

Find a kitchen hand to help you prepare the ingredients ahead of time

Pre-heat your oven to 180°C (350°F) at least 20 minutes before cooking and position an oven tray in the middle shelf of the oven

Equipment:

Measuring jug — Measuring spoons — Sharp knife — Chopping board — Scales — Whisk — Grater — Medium mixing bowl — Metal skewer — Metal tablespoon — Oven mitts — Sifter — Kitchen scissors — 12 paper cases — 12-hole muffin tin

Herb and garlic bread

This is perfect as a quick, indulgent snack –
and just as nice as an entrée to a meal.
It's super-rich though, so don't go eating it
every day!

Makes 24 slices

Prep time: 20 minutes

Cooking time: 20–30 minutes

Ingredients

3 large cloves of garlic, finely grated
   or crushed
250 g (9 oz) salted butter, softened and
   cut into 2 cm (¾ in) cubes
1 tablespoon olive oil
1 teaspoon dried oregano
1 pinch finely ground black pepper
1 tablespoon firmly packed fresh
   parsley leaves
6 chives
1 large baguette, cut on the diagonal into
   twenty-four 2 cm (¾ in) thick slices

Method

Position a rack at the top of your grill (broiler) and pre-heat
on high.

Put the garlic, butter, oil, oregano and pepper into the bowl
of a food processor. Using scissors, finely snip in the parsley
and chives. Place the lid on your food processor and combine
the mixture until smooth, roughly 1–2 minutes. Use a bowl
scraper to scrape down the sides as you go.

With adult help: Turn the processor off at the power outlet
and remove the processor blade. Use a butter knife to spread
the butter mixture on both sides of the bread slices.

With adult help: Arrange the buttered bread on a baking
tray and place under the pre-heated grill for 3 minutes, or
until lightly golden. Wearing oven mitts, use tongs to turn
the bread over and repeat for the other side. Use tongs to
transfer to a serving platter and enjoy immediately!

To make a garlic and herb butter log:
Tear off a 40 cm (16 in) long piece of baking paper and lay
on a clean work surface.

Make the garlic and herb butter according to the method
above. Once the butter has been processed until smooth and
an adult has removed the processor blade, use a bowl scraper
to scoop out the butter and form a 20 cm (8 in) long log on
the baking paper. Roll the butter log up and twist the ends of
the paper tightly so it resembles a giant wrapped lolly.

Refrigerate until firm, then keep in your freezer for up to a
month. Slice off rounds of butter as you need them. Let the
butter come to room temperature before spreading.

Equipment:

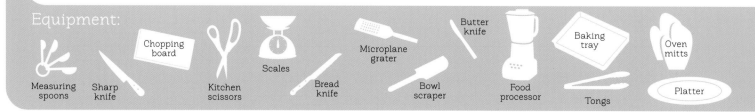

Measuring spoons   Sharp knife   Chopping board   Kitchen scissors   Scales   Bread knife   Microplane grater   Bowl scraper   Butter knife   Food processor   Baking tray   Tongs   Oven mitts   Platter

Time-saving tips

Have all your equipment and ingredients ready

Find a kitchen hand to help you prepare the ingredients ahead of time

Make a garlic and herb butter log in advance, for garlic bread at any time

Sloppy Joes

Don't let the name put you off – these burgers might be messy to eat, but they're very tasty! Satisfy your craving for fast food with this healthier, homemade option: enjoy with a side of coleslaw and fries.

> Serves 2

> Prep time: 20 minutes

> Cooking time: 30 minutes

Ingredients

1 tablespoon olive oil

1 small onion, finely chopped

1 large garlic clove, finely grated
  or crushed

200 g (7 oz) very lean minced
  (ground) beef

2 tablespoons tomato sauce (ketchup)

1 teaspoon red wine vinegar

1 tablespoon soft brown sugar

2 tablespoons American mustard

2 pinches chilli powder

1 teaspoon sea salt

1 pinch finely ground black pepper

2 round white bread rolls, sliced in half

2 small pickled gherkins, thinly sliced
  lengthways

Method

Preheat your oven to 180°C (350°F).

With adult help: Heat the olive oil in a frying pan over medium heat. Add the onion and garlic and cook, stirring regularly, until golden, about 2–3 minutes. Add the beef mince and fry until it is just cooked, roughly 1–2 minutes. Keep stirring to prevent sticking. Add the tomato sauce, vinegar, sugar, mustard, chilli, salt and pepper. Cook, stirring well, for about 2 minutes.

With adult help: Wearing oven mitts, place the bread rolls, cut-side down, on a baking tray in the middle shelf of the oven. Heat for 3 minutes, then remove, once more wearing oven mitts.

Evenly spoon the beef mince into the bread rolls. Top with the pickled gherkin slices and the bread 'lids'. Serve immediately.

Time-saving tips

Have all your equipment and ingredients ready

Find a kitchen hand to help you prepare the ingredients ahead of time

Pre-heat your oven to 180°C (350°F) at least 20 minutes before cooking

Have an oven tray positioned in the middle shelf of the oven

Equipment:

Scales — Measuring spoons — Chopping board — Sharp knife — Microplane grater — Metal kitchen spoon — Frying pan — Oven mitts

white
roll

savoury
mince

gherkins

Panzanella (Italian torn-bread salad)

Panzanella is a traditional Italian salad from Tuscany. It's packed with flavour and works equally well as a snack or as a side dish.

Serves 4 as a side dish

Prep time: 30 minutes

Cooking time: 20 minutes

Ingredients

1 x 300 g (10½ oz) rustic bread loaf, such
   as casalinga or ciabatta, torn into 3 cm
   (1¼ in) pieces
2 garlic cloves
400 g (14 oz) assorted small tomatoes,
   such as cherry and grape tomatoes,
   sliced in half
2 tablespoons firmly packed fresh
   basil leaves
50 g (1¾ oz) capers, rinsed and
   squeezed dry
3 tablespoons olive oil
2 teaspoons red wine vinegar
1 teaspoon lemon juice
1½ teaspoons sea salt
¼ red onion, finely diced

Method

Pre-heat your grill (broiler) to high. Arrange the bread pieces in one layer on a baking tray.

With adult help: Toast the bread under a hot grill for 3 minutes. Wearing oven mitts and using tongs, turn the bread over, then grill for a further 3–4 minutes, or until lightly golden.

While the bread is toasting, grate or crush the garlic into a large serving bowl. Add in the remaining ingredients and mix well.

With adult help: Wearing oven mitts, remove the baking tray from the grill. Using tongs, add the toasted bread to the salad and combine well. Best served immediately, while the bread is still crunchy!

Time-saving tips

Have all your equipment and ingredients ready

Find a kitchen hand to help you prepare the ingredients ahead of time

Pre-heat your grill (broiler) on high at least 10 minutes before cooking

Equipment:

 Scales
 Measuring spoons
 Sharp knife
Chopping board
 Large kitchen spoon
 Microplane grater
 Baking tray
 Large non-reactive serving bowl
Oven mitts
Tongs

cherry
tomato

grilled
bread

fresh
basil

Macerated strawberries in balsamic

Strawberries and balsamic vinegar might sound like a strange flavour combination, but it actually works really well – trust me! This is delicious served with vanilla cream or ice cream.

Serves 4

Prep time: 15-20 minutes

Cooking time: 30 minutes

Ingredients

2 tablespoons balsamic vinegar glaze
  (see Note)
2 tablespoons caster (superfine) sugar
500 g (1 lb 2 oz) ripe strawberries, hulled
  and quartered
200 ml (7 fl oz) thickened (whipping)
  cream
1 teaspoon natural vanilla extract
8 mint leaves

Method

Whisk the balsamic vinegar glaze and sugar in a non-reactive mixing bowl. Add the strawberries and combine well, using a large spoon, then allow to stand, or macerate, in a cool place for roughly 20 minutes.

While the strawberries are macerating, put the cream and vanilla extract in the bowl of an electric mixer and whip on high until soft peaks form.

Spoon the strawberries into serving bowls and use a spoon to dollop the vanilla cream on top. Garnish with mint leaves and enjoy.

Note

Balsamic vinegar glaze or syrup can be found in gourmet food stores and some major supermarkets.

Time-saving tips

Have all your equipment and ingredients ready

Find a kitchen hand to help you prepare the ingredients ahead of time

Equipment:

Measuring spoons

Measuring jug

Chopping board

Sharp knife

Scales

Medium non-reactive mixing bowl

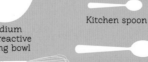
Whisk

Kitchen spoon

Large metal kitchen spoon

Electric mixer

4 spoons

4 serving bowls

fresh mint

strawberry

balsamic
glaze

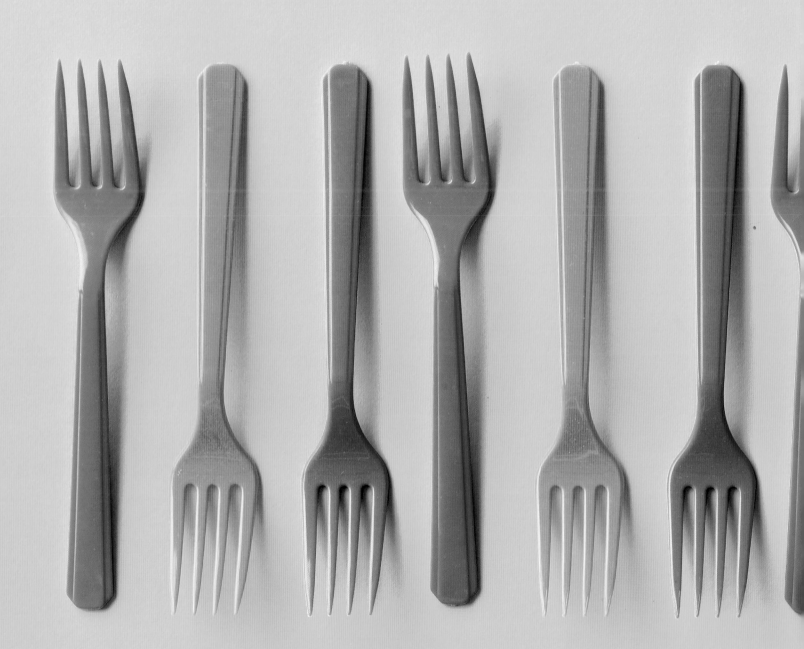

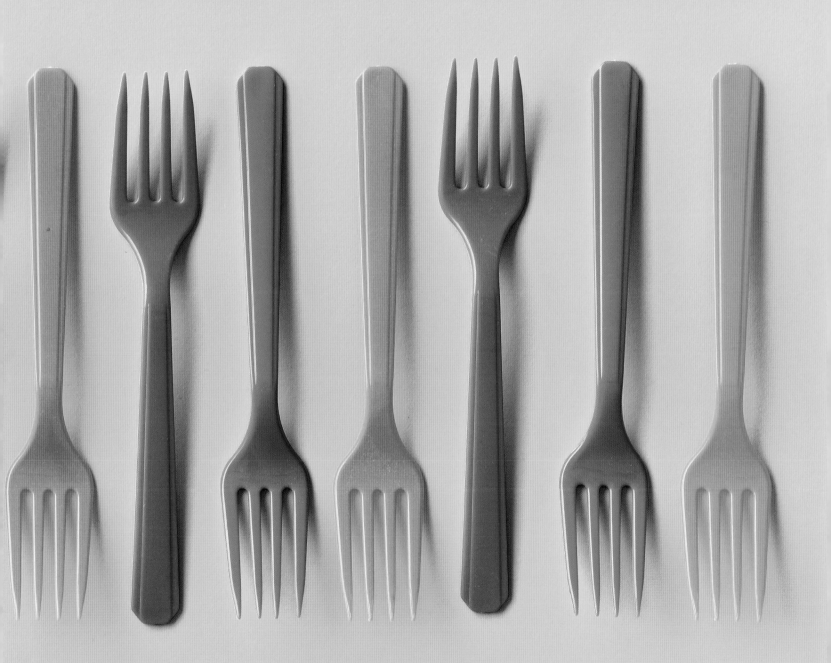

Lemon curd

I love lemon curd – it somehow manages to be rich *and* fruity at the same time. You can make all kinds of different curds using tart fruit juices. Enjoy with meringues, scones, cakes or even on toast!

Makes about 1 cup

Prep time: 20 minutes

Cooking time: 30 minutes

Ingredients

70 g (2½ oz) caster (superfine) sugar
2 egg yolks
3 eggs
50 ml (1¾ fl oz) lemon juice (from
  roughly 1 medium lemon)
100 g (3½ oz) unsalted butter,
  roughly chopped

Method

In a mixing bowl, whisk together the sugar, egg yolks and whole eggs until frothy. Set aside.

With adult help: Put the lemon juice and butter in a saucepan and melt over medium heat. When the butter has melted, reduce the heat to low. Pour the egg mixture into the saucepan and whisk continuously until the mixture thickly coats the back of a wooden spoon, about 5 minutes.

With adult help: Remove the saucepan from the heat. Pour the curd into a strainer over a clean mixing bowl, using a tablespoon to push the curd through. This removes any accidental eggy clumps that may have formed during cooking. Chill until needed.

Time-saving tips

Have all your equipment and ingredients ready

Find a kitchen hand to help you prepare the ingredients ahead of time

Equipment:

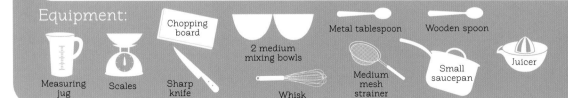

Measuring jug • Scales • Chopping board • Sharp knife • 2 medium mixing bowls • Whisk • Metal tablespoon • Wooden spoon • Medium mesh strainer • Small saucepan • Juicer

raspberries

lemon
curd

meringue

passionfruit

Ricotta hotcakes

Lighter than normal hotcakes thanks to the addition of ricotta, these beauties will impress everybody! You can serve these with a sweet topping or a savoury one – try maple syrup with crisp bacon, in true American style!

Makes 8

Prep time: 20 minutes

Cooking time: 20–30 minutes

Ingredients

110 g (4 oz/¾ cup) plain (all-purpose) flour

½ teaspoon bicarbonate of soda
  (baking soda)

½ teaspoon baking powder

1 egg

200 ml (7 fl oz) milk

½ teaspoon white vinegar

40 g (1½ oz/2 tablespoons) unsalted
  butter, melted and cooled slightly

1 pinch sea salt

200 g (7 oz) fresh ricotta

2 teaspoons softened unsalted butter,
  for frying

Ice cream and maple syrup, to serve
  (optional)

Method

Sift the flour, bicarbonate of soda and baking powder into a large mixing bowl and set aside. Crack the egg into a medium mixing bowl and add the milk, vinegar, melted butter, salt and ricotta, and whisk until smooth. Carefully pour the wet ingredients into the dry and combine well. Set aside.

With adult help: Heat the frying pan over a medium–low heat. Using a pastry brush, grease the frying pan with one teaspoon of softened butter. Measure 60 ml (2 fl oz/¼ cup) of hotcake batter and carefully pour it into the frying pan, trying to make the batter form a circular shape. Repeat 3 more times. Cook until bubbles appear in the hotcakes, about 3 minutes – this means the hotcakes are cooked on one side.

With adult help: Use the spatula to carefully flip the hotcakes over and cook for a further 2–3 minutes on the other side. Once the hotcakes are ready, transfer them to a serving platter using the spatula. Repeat the frying steps for the final four hotcakes and enjoy while hot.

Time-saving tips

Have all your equipment and ingredients ready

Find a kitchen hand to help you prepare the ingredients ahead of time

Equipment:

Measuring cups

Measuring spoons

Sifter

Measuring jug

Scales

2 mixing bowls

Large frying pan

Spatula

Whisk

Pastry brush

Platter

Peanut cookies

I'm a huge fan of any dessert that mixes sweet and salty flavours – and these cookies do just that. Using biscuit (cookie) flour isn't essential, but it makes the biscuits just that little bit lighter.

Makes approximately 50
Prep time: 20 minutes
Cooking time: 30 minutes

Ingredients

110 g (4 oz) unsalted butter, softened
45 g (1½ oz/¼ cup lightly packed) dark
    brown sugar
1 egg
120 g (4¼ oz/1 cup less 1 tablespoon)
    self-raising cake and biscuit (cookie) flour
60 g (2 oz/⅓ cup) crushed peanuts
½ teaspoon salt
1 pinch cinnamon
50 salted peanut halves, for garnish

Method

Pre-heat your oven to 180ºC (350ºF). Line both baking trays with baking paper.

Put all of the ingredients except for the peanut halves in the bowl of an electric mixer. Mix on medium–high until just combined, scraping down the sides of the bowl with a bowl scraper as you go. Refrigerate mixture for 5–10 minutes.

Take a teaspoon of cookie batter and roll it into a ball with clean hands. Place it on one of the lined baking trays and repeat until all the batter has been used, leaving a 6 cm (2¼ in) space between each cookie. With two fingers, gently flatten the top of each cookie, then press a peanut half into the centre.

With adult help: Wearing oven mitts, place the baking trays in the oven on the middle and lower shelves. Bake the cookies for 6 minutes – no longer! Remove the trays from the oven with oven mitts and allow the cookies to cool for 2 minutes.

Using a spatula, remove the cookies from the tray and place on a wire rack. Serve when cooled slightly, or keep for up to 1 week in an airtight container.

Time-saving tips

Have all your equipment and ingredients ready

Find a kitchen hand to help you prepare the ingredients ahead of time

Pre-heat your oven to 180ºC (350ºF) 20 minutes before cooking and have oven trays positioned in the middle and lower shelves of the oven

Equipment:

 Measuring spoons

 Scales

 Chopping board / Sharp knife

 Baking paper

 Bowl scraper

 Electric mixer

 Oven mitts / Spatula

 Wire rack

Mont Blanc

This dessert, also known as 'Monte Bianco' in Italian, is made to look like a snow-capped mountain, specifically Mont Blanc in France. Make this just before serving, so the meringue stays crunchy.

Serves 4
Prep time: 20 minutes
Cooking time: 20 minutes

Ingredients

125 g (4½ oz) ginger nut biscuits
   (ginger snap cookies)
300 ml (10 fl oz) thickened (whipping)
   cream
1½ teaspoons natural vanilla extract
40 g (1½ oz/approximately 3) ready-made
   meringue nests
200 g (7 oz) ready-made sweetened
   chestnut jam (see Note)
4 chocolate curls or chocolate shavings,
   optional

Method

Place the biscuits into the bowl of a food processor and process for about 40 seconds, or until you obtain a sand-like consistency.

With adult help: Turn the processor off at the power outlet and remove the processor blade. Using a spoon, divide the biscuit 'rubble' equally between four dessert glasses.

Place the cream and vanilla in the bowl of an electric mixer and whip it on high until soft peaks form, about 40 seconds. Using clean hands, crumble two meringue nests into the mixture and stir to combine well. Set aside.

Evenly dollop the chestnut jam in each of the glasses, followed by the cream and meringue mixture. Crumble the remaining meringue over the top and garnish with a chocolate curl or chocolate shavings, if you like. Enjoy immediately!

Note

Sweetened chestnut jam comes in cans or jars and can be found in Italian supermarkets or gourmet food stores.

Time-saving tips

Have all your equipment and ingredients ready

Find a kitchen hand to help you prepare the ingredients ahead of time

Equipment:

Measuring spoons

Measuring jug

Scales

Food processor

Electric mixer

Kitchen spoon

4 dessert glasses

4 dessert spoons

whipped
cream

crumbly
meringue

chestnut
jam

Bigger Bites

Recipes you can cook
in 30 minutes or more

Tomato and basil bruschetta

This is a dish my mum used to make in Italy, her home country. She passed this recipe on to me years ago and I've made it ever since.

Serves 2
Prep time: 30 minutes
Cooking time: 30 minutes

Ingredients

2 slices of sourdough bread, about 2 cm
(¾ in) thick, cut on the diagonal
1½ tablespoons olive oil
1 medium garlic clove, halved
2 large, ripe Roma tomatoes, cut into
1 cm (½ inch) cubes
¼ small red (Spanish) onion, finely diced
½ teaspoon red wine vinegar
¼ teaspoon sea salt
2 pinches finely ground black pepper
1 tablespoon firmly packed fresh
basil leaves

Method

With adult help: Pre-heat your chargrill pan over high heat.

Brush both sides of the bread with a ½ tablespoon of the olive oil.

With adult help: Toast the bread on the chargrill pan for about 3 minutes each side, using tongs to flip the bread over. When ready, your toast should have charred grill marks on it.

Transfer the toast to a chopping board using tongs. While the toast is still a little warm, rub the cut side of the garlic all over one side of each slice. Place on a serving platter and set aside.

Combine the tomatoes, remaining olive oil, onion, vinegar, salt, pepper and basil in a non-reactive mixing bowl. Check for seasoning, then evenly spoon the tomato topping onto the slices of toast. Serve immediately.

Time-saving tips

Have all your equipment and ingredients ready

Find a kitchen hand to help you prepare the ingredients ahead of time

Pre-heat your chargrill pan ahead of time

Equipment:

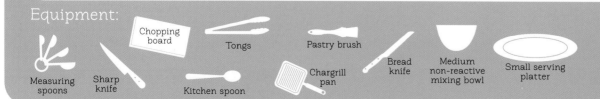

Measuring spoons
Sharp knife
Chopping board
Kitchen spoon
Tongs
Chargrill pan
Pastry brush
Bread knife
Medium non-reactive mixing bowl
Small serving platter

chopped
tomatoes

grilled
bread

fresh
basil

Lemon and tuna orzo

This recipe is so easy to prepare – perfect for when you want to make your family an easy, no-fuss dinner. Just double the recipe to serve four people.

Serves 2
Prep time: 30 minutes
Cooking time: 30 minutes

Ingredients

1 tablespoon salt, to add to pasta water

200 g (7 oz) orzo or risoni pasta

60 g (2 oz/3 tablespoons) salted butter

1 garlic clove, finely grated

130 g (4½ oz) tinned tuna in oil, drained and flaked

1 teaspoon lemon juice

2 teaspoons flat-leaf (Italian) parsley leaves

10 g (¼ oz) parmesan cheese

Method

With adult help: Add one tablespoon of salt to a large saucepan and fill it three-quarters of the way up with water you have boiled in a kettle. Heat the salted water over high heat until boiling, then, wearing oven mitts, carefully add orzo to the pot. Watch for splashing. Cook orzo uncovered for ten minutes or until al dente (cooked through but still firm), stirring regularly to prevent sticking.

With adult help: Meanwhile, melt the butter in a medium saucepan over medium heat. Add the grated garlic and fry for 30 seconds. Add the tuna, lemon juice and parsley leaves and heat through.

With adult help: Wearing oven mitts, drain the cooked orzo by pouring it into a colander placed in the sink. Add the orzo to the tuna mixture and stir through before dividing between 2 bowls.

Using a speed peeler, evenly shave the parmesan over the orzo. Serve immediately.

Time-saving tips

Have all your equipment and ingredients ready

Find a kitchen hand to help you prepare the ingredients ahead of time

Boil and salt your pasta water while you prepare your ingredients

Equipment:

 Measuring spoons

 Juicer

 Chopping board

 Sharp knife

 Scales

 Microplane grater

 Large saucepan

 Kettle

 Long-handled wooden spoon

 Colander

 Oven mitts

 Medium saucepan / Speed peeler

 2 serving bowls

Fancy chicken sandwiches

These chicken sandwiches are a cinch to make and perfect for parties. You could also whip up a smaller batch for lunch or as an after-school treat!

Makes 32 sandwiches
Prep time: 20-25 minutes
Cooking time: 25-30 minutes

Ingredients

24 chives

½ medium roast chicken, skin discarded, meat removed and finely shredded (approximately 260 g/9 oz meat)

125 g (4½ oz/½ cup) whole-egg mayonnaise

1 tablespoon dijon mustard

½ teaspoon salt

2 pinches pepper

16 slices of white bread, crusts removed

To garnish

3 tablespoons sesame seeds

2 tablespoons whole-egg mayonnaise

10 chives, finely chopped

Method

Using scissors, finely snip the chives into a medium mixing bowl. Add the chicken, ½ cup of mayonnaise, mustard, salt and pepper. Combine well with a spoon.

Arrange 8 slices of bread on a clean work surface and, using a small bowl scraper, evenly spread on the chicken mixture. Top with the remaining slices of bread.

With adult help: Using a sharp knife, cut each sandwich into 4 small triangles. Try not to squash the sandwiches too much!

Put the sesame seeds on a small, flat plate. Using a pastry brush, thinly brush one edge of each sandwich triangle with the remaining mayonnaise. Press that side into the sesame seeds, then place on a serving platter. Sprinkle over extra chives and serve immediately.

Note

Although these sandwiches are best eaten fresh, they can be made 1 hour in advance and kept, wrapped in plastic wrap, in the refrigerator.

Time-saving tips

Have all your equipment and ingredients ready

Find a kitchen hand to help you prepare the ingredients ahead of time

---

Equipment:

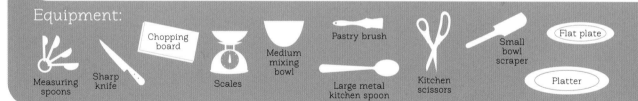

Measuring spoons · Sharp knife · Chopping board · Scales · Medium mixing bowl · Pastry brush · Large metal kitchen spoon · Kitchen scissors · Small bowl scraper · Flat plate · Platter

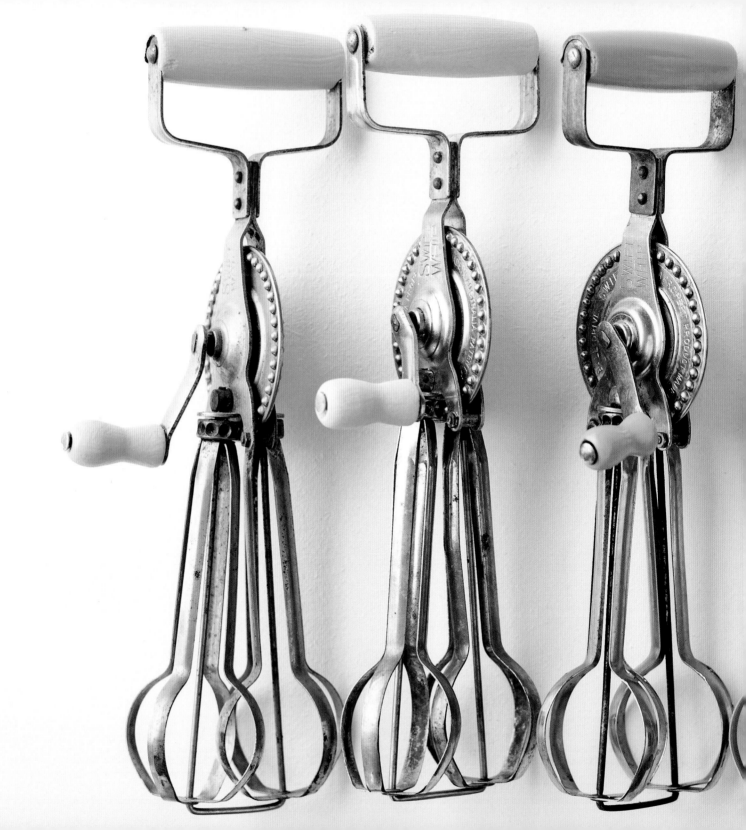

Chicken and sweetcorn soup

My husband taught me how to make this soup more than a decade ago! It's comforting and perfect enjoyed on a cold day.

Serves 4 or 7 as an entrée
Prep time: 30 minutes +
Cooking time: 30 minutes +

Ingredients

1 tablespoon sesame oil
1 cm (½ in) piece fresh ginger, finely grated
2 spring onions (scallions), finely sliced
150 g (5½ oz) creamed corn
100 g (3½ oz) corn kernels (fresh or canned)
1 litre (34 fl oz/4 cups) chicken stock (see Notes)
1 teaspoon salt
1 pinch finely ground white pepper
1 egg, beaten well
80 g (2¾ oz) finely shredded roast chicken breast fillet
35 g (1¼ oz/¼ cup) fried shallots, to garnish (see Notes)
1 spring onion (scallion), sliced on the diagonal, to garnish

Method

With adult help: Pour the sesame oil into a large saucepan and heat over medium heat. Add the ginger and spring onion, and stir well. Carefully add the corn, chicken stock, salt and pepper. Bring to the boil then reduce the heat to low and simmer with the lid slightly askew.

With adult help: After 20 minutes, turn the heat off, add the beaten egg and carefully whisk for 10 seconds. Turn the heat back on, add the chicken breast to the soup and cook for 20 seconds, then check for seasoning. Evenly ladle the soup into bowls, top with fried shallots and spring onion and serve immediately.

Notes

If using stock cubes, I recommend using 1½ cubes in 1 litre (34 fl oz/4 cups) of water.

Fried shallots can be found in Asian supermarkets and in the international food aisle of some major supermarkets.

Time-saving tips

Have all your equipment and ingredients ready

Find a kitchen hand to help you prepare the ingredients ahead of time

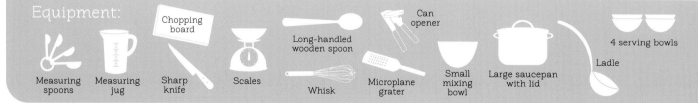

Equipment: Measuring spoons · Measuring jug · Chopping board · Sharp knife · Scales · Long-handled wooden spoon · Whisk · Microplane grater · Can opener · Small mixing bowl · Large saucepan with lid · Ladle · 4 serving bowls

Croque monsieur

This fancy toasted sandwich is what French people consider fast food! Croque monsieur's crunchy, buttery outside and oozy cheesy inside make it the ultimate comfort food.

Serves 2

Prep time: 20 minutes

Cooking time: 30 minutes

Ingredients

50 g (1¾ oz) gruyère cheese, grated
1 tablespoon crème fraîche
1 teaspoon dijon mustard
20 g (¾ oz/1 tablespoon) butter, softened
4 slices of bread, such as sourdough
  casalinga, about 1.5 cm (½ in) thick
70 g (2½ oz) shaved ham

Method

In a mixing bowl, combine gruyère, crème fraîche and mustard.

On a chopping board, butter one side of each of the bread slices. Turn them over to reveal the unbuttered side and, using a small bowl scraper, cover each slice with the cheese mixture right to the edges. Place the ham on two slices and tuck in as neatly as possible, then top with the remaining slices of bread.

With adult help: Heat a frying pan on medium heat for 30 seconds. Using a spatula, carefully place the sandwiches into the frying pan. Fry until lightly golden, about 3 minutes. Wearing an oven mitt and using the spatula, carefully flip sandwiches over and fry until lightly golden on the second side.

With adult help: With the spatula, press down firmly on each sandwich for 30 seconds to stick the two sides together. Cook for another 2–3 minutes, until golden-brown, then transfer the sandwiches onto plates.

Use a pizza cutter to slice sandwiches in half and serve immediately.

Time-saving tips

Have all your equipment and ingredients ready

Find a kitchen hand to help you prepare the ingredients ahead of time

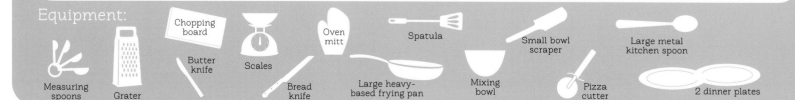

Equipment:

Measuring spoons · Grater · Chopping board · Butter knife · Scales · Bread knife · Oven mitt · Large heavy-based frying pan · Spatula · Mixing bowl · Small bowl scraper · Pizza cutter · Large metal kitchen spoon · 2 dinner plates

gooey
cheese
filling

toasted
bread

shaved
ham

Tomato and basil penne

One of my best friends, Emily, taught me how to make a variation of this recipe over a decade ago. I love how this dish is bursting with summery freshness.

Serves 4 kids

Prep time: 30 minutes

Cooking time: 30 minutes

Ingredients

1 tablespoon salt, to add to pasta water
300 g (10½ oz) penne
2 tablespoons olive oil
1 kg (2 lb 3 oz) ripe tomatoes, stem ends removed, sliced into wedges
1½ tablespoons sea salt
10 g (¼ oz/⅓ cup) torn fresh basil leaves
1 teaspoon flat-leaf (Italian) parsley leaves
40 g (1½ oz/¼ cup) toasted pine nuts
Marinated goat's cheese or parmesan cheese, to garnish, optional

Method

With adult help: Add one tablespoon of salt to a large saucepan and fill it three-quarters of the way up with water you have boiled in a kettle. Heat the salted water over high heat until boiling, then, wearing oven mitts, carefully add the penne. Stir regularly with a long-handled wooden spoon to prevent the pasta sticking. Cook for 12 minutes, or until al dente (cooked through but still firm).

With adult help: While the pasta is cooking, heat the oil in a large frying pan over medium–low heat. Wearing oven mitts, add the tomato and salt to the pan, being careful of splashing. Cook, with the lid askew and stirring occasionally, until the tomatoes have been reduced to a chunky sauce, around 15 minutes. Stir in the basil and parsley.

With adult help: Wearing oven mitts, pour the cooked penne into a colander positioned in the sink and drain well. Return the penne to the saucepan, add the sauce and stir well. Heat through over medium heat for roughly 1 minute.

Divide between 4 bowls and serve immediately with a sprinkling of toasted pine nuts. If you like, place a bowl of marinated goat's cheese or shaved parmesan cheese on the table – invite everyone to take a little and crumble or scatter over their pasta.

Time-saving tips

Have all your equipment and ingredients ready

Find a kitchen hand to help you prepare the ingredients ahead of time

Equipment:

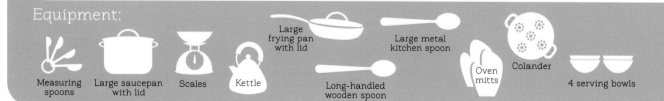

Measuring spoons | Large saucepan with lid | Scales | Kettle | Large frying pan with lid | Long-handled wooden spoon | Large metal kitchen spoon | Oven mitts | Colander | 4 serving bowls

fresh
basil

goat's
cheese

penne

Little tuna and tomato tartlets

These tartlets are great for a party, as an entrée or even as a quick after-school snack. You can vary the filling in these tarts – try experimenting with different flavour combinations!

Makes 9 tartlets

Prep time: 30 minutes

Cooking time: 30 minutes +

Ingredients

1 teaspoon butter
3 x 24 cm (9½ in) squares ready-made
   puff pastry, thawed
2 eggs
185 g (6½ oz) tinned tuna in oil
70 g (2½ oz) cheddar cheese, grated
½ small onion, finely diced
1 large garlic clove, finely grated
   or crushed
125 ml (4½ fl oz/½ cup) cream
1 teaspoon salt
½ teaspoon finely ground black pepper
10 chives, finely chopped
1 tomato, sliced thinly into 9 rounds

Method

Pre-heat your oven to 200°C (430°F). Using some scrunched-up baking paper, grease a standard 9-hole muffin tin with butter.

To make pastry rounds, turn a 9 cm (3½ in) diameter bowl upside-down and press it firmly into the pastry square, twisting back and forth. Peel the round away from the backing sheet and repeat until you have 9 rounds. Place one pastry round in each muffin-tin hole. Prick the pastry a few times with a fork, then place a 10 cm (4 in) square of baking paper on top of each round. Place pie weights, dried beans or uncooked rice on top of the baking paper pieces.

With adult help: Wearing oven mitts, place the muffin tin on the middle shelf of your oven and bake for 10 minutes, or until the pastry is puffed and golden. Remove the pastry cases from the oven, once more wearing oven mitts. Remove the pie weights and baking paper but leave the pastry in the tin.

While the pastry cases are baking, crack the eggs into a medium mixing bowl and whisk until frothy. Add the tuna, cheese, onion, garlic, cream, salt, pepper and chives, then mix well. Spoon the egg mixture evenly into the pastry cases and top each with a tomato round.

With adult help: Wearing oven mitts, return the muffin tin to the middle shelf of the oven. Bake for around 25 minutes. The tarts are ready when the filling springs back slightly when gently pressed with a spoon – no liquid should come out. Once more wearing oven mitts, remove the tin from the oven. Run a butter knife around the edge of each tartlet to loosen them, then gently remove the tarts from the tin using tongs. Serve immediately!

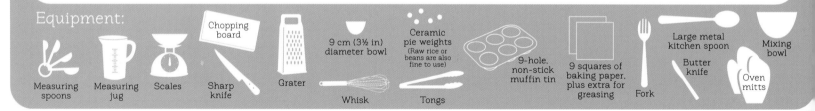

Equipment: Measuring spoons · Measuring jug · Scales · Sharp knife · Chopping board · Grater · 9 cm (3½ in) diameter bowl · Whisk · Ceramic pie weights (Raw rice or beans are also fine to use) · Tongs · 9-hole, non-stick muffin tin · 9 squares of baking paper, plus extra for greasing · Fork · Large metal kitchen spoon · Butter knife · Oven mitts · Mixing bowl

Time-saving tips

Have all your equipment and ingredients ready

Find a kitchen hand to help you prepare the
ingredients ahead of time

Pre-heat your oven to 200ºC (430ºF) at least
20 minutes before cooking

Have an oven tray positioned in the middle shelf of
the oven

Have the pastry thawed in advance

Chicken satay skewers

Satay is one of my favourite flavours ever!
I recommend soaking your skewers before
cooking to stop them from burning.

| Makes 8 small (half-size) skewers |
| Prep time: 30 minutes + |
| Cooking time: 30 minutes + |

Ingredients

350 g (12½ oz) chicken breast fillets,
  cut into 2 cm (¾ in) cubes
2 tablespoons vegetable oil
1 small onion, very finely diced
1 garlic clove, finely grated
1 pinch chilli powder
100 ml (3½ fl oz) water
100 g (3½ oz) crunchy peanut butter
½ teaspoon lime juice
1½ tablespoons finely grated palm sugar
  (jaggery), or soft brown sugar
2 teaspoons tamari
1 teaspoon sea salt
1 x 2 cm (¾ in) piece ginger, finely grated
2 tablespoons vegetable oil, for frying

Method

Thread the chicken cubes onto the skewers. Place the skewers
into a 30 cm x 40 cm (12 in x 16 in) baking dish and set aside.

With adult help: Heat the vegetable oil in a small frying pan
over medium heat. Add the onion, garlic and chilli, and fry,
stirring constantly, for 2 minutes, or until golden. Reduce the
heat to low. Add the water, peanut butter, lime juice, sugar,
tamari, ginger and salt. Stir well and cook for another 2
minutes. Allow to cool.

Pour the cooled satay sauce over the chicken skewers and
use a wooden spoon to spread evenly. With tongs, turn each
skewer over to coat it in sauce. Leave the chicken to marinate
for at least 5 minutes. If you have more time, marinate the
chicken longer – the flavour will become even better!

With adult help: Heat the remaining oil in a large frying
pan over medium–low heat. Wearing oven mitts and using
tongs, put the skewers into the pan. Make sure you stand
well back, as the oil can spatter. Cook the satay skewers for
roughly 4 minutes each side, using clean tongs to turn them
over. Once the chicken is cooked, transfer the skewers to a
platter and serve immediately with satay sauce on the side.

Time-saving tips

Have all your equipment and ingredients ready

Find a kitchen hand to help you prepare the
ingredients ahead of time

Soak the bamboo skewers in advance

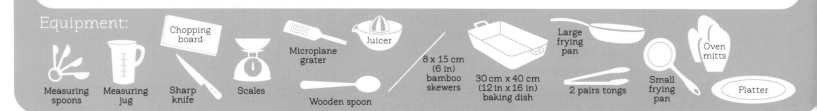

Equipment: Measuring spoons · Measuring jug · Chopping board · Sharp knife · Scales · Microplane grater · Wooden spoon · Juicer · 8 x 15 cm (6 in) bamboo skewers · 30 cm x 40 cm (12 in x 16 in) baking dish · Large frying pan · 2 pairs tongs · Small frying pan · Oven mitts · Platter

marinated
chicken

spicy satay
sauce

Pumpkin soup

This is a hearty dish perfect for warming you up on cold autumn or winter nights. You could also serve it at Halloween – use the pumpkin left over from carving jack-o'-lanterns.

Serves 4

Prep time: 30 minutes +

Cooking time: 30 minutes +

Ingredients

2 tablespoons olive oil

1 large onion, halved

2 large garlic cloves, halved

1 celery stick, leaves removed, sliced in half

500 g butternut pumpkin (squash), peeled, seeded and cut into 3 cm (1¼ in) cubes

750 ml (25½ fl oz/3 cups) vegetable stock (see Note)

1 teaspoon sea salt

1 pinch finely ground black pepper

250 ml (8½ fl oz/1 cup) milk

1 spring onion (scallion), sliced diagonally, to garnish

Method

With adult help: Heat the olive oil in a large saucepan over medium heat. Add the onion, garlic, celery and pumpkin and fry until lightly golden, about 5 minutes. Stir well to prevent sticking. Once the vegetables are ready, carefully pour in the stock and add salt and pepper. Increase the heat to medium–high and simmer with the lid askew for 20 minutes, or until the vegetables are soft. Use a wooden spoon to squash a piece of pumpkin to check if it's cooked.

With adult help: Turn the heat off and allow the soup to cool slightly. Wearing oven mitts and using a stick blender on the lowest setting, blend the soup until it is completely smooth. Be careful, as steam will escape from the saucepan as you do this. Add milk and stir well.

With adult help: Reheat the soup until simmering, about 1 minute. Once it is heated through, ladle into bowls, sprinkle with spring onion and serve immediately.

Note

If using stock cubes, I recommend using 1 cube in 750 ml (25½ fl oz/3 cups) of water.

Time-saving tips
Have all your equipment and ingredients ready
Find a kitchen hand to help you prepare the ingredients ahead of time

Equipment:

 Measuring spoons

Measuring jug

 Chopping board

 Sharp knife

 Scales

 Long-handled wooden spoon

 Large saucepan with lid

 Oven mitts

Ladle

 Stick blender

 4 serving bowls

Potato and bacon hash

Potato hash was one of my favourite recipes to make when I was younger. I sometimes finely grate my potatoes using a coarse microplane grater – this ensures that the hashes cook evenly inside and out!

Makes 14

Prep time: 30 minutes +

Cooking time: 30 minutes +

Ingredients

300 g (10½ oz) potatoes, peeled and
   finely grated using a food processor
   with grater attachment
4 spring onions (scallions)
4 chives
1 egg
35 g (1¼ oz/¼ cup) plain (all-purpose)
   flour
130 g (4½ oz) bacon, crisp-cooked,
   fat removed, finely diced
½ teaspoon salt
1 teaspoon finely ground black pepper
2 tablespoons vegetable oil

Method

Put the grated potato in a large mixing bowl. Using a clean tea towel, forcefully scrunch the potato to soak up as much starchy liquid as you can. Repeat with another clean tea towel.

Using scissors, finely snip the spring onions and chives into the bowl. Crack in the egg, then add the flour, bacon, salt and pepper. Using a kitchen spoon, combine well.

Scoop out a ¼ cup of the potato mixture and shape it into a round, flat patty. Place the patty on one of the baking trays and repeat until all of the mixture is used up.

On the other baking tray, layer 2 large pieces of kitchen towel.

With adult help: Heat 1 tablespoon of oil in a large frying pan over high heat. Using a spatula, place half of the patties into the frying pan and fry for 1 minute on each side. Reduce the heat to medium-low and cook for a further 2–3 minutes on each side, flattening the patties with your spatula to help them cook through.

With adult help: Carefully remove the patties from the pan and place on the paper towel to soak up any extra oil. Repeat until all the patties are cooked, then serve immediately.

Time-saving tips

Have all your equipment and ingredients ready

Find a kitchen hand to help you prepare the ingredients ahead of time

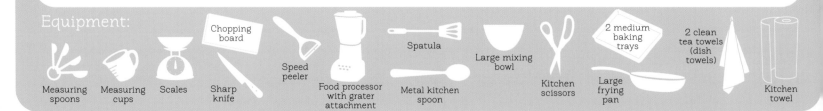

Equipment:

Measuring spoons · Measuring cups · Scales · Sharp knife · Speed peeler · Food processor with grater attachment · Chopping board · Metal kitchen spoon · Spatula · Large mixing bowl · Kitchen scissors · Large frying pan · 2 medium baking trays · 2 clean tea towels (dish towels) · Kitchen towel

Cheesy mac

This is my idea of comfort food! It's great enjoyed now and again, to satisfy that craving for something rich and creamy.

Serves 6
Prep time: 15-20 minutes
Cooking time: 25-30 minutes

Ingredients

1 tablespoon salt, to add to pasta water
350 g (12½ oz) macaroni
40 g (1½ oz/2 tablespoons) salted butter
3 tablespoons plain (all-purpose) flour
500 ml (17 fl oz/2 cups) milk
100 g (3½ oz) cheddar cheese, grated
1 pinch ground nutmeg
1 pinch finely ground black pepper
½ teaspoon sweet paprika
½ teaspoon sea salt
1 tablespoon firmly packed and finely
   chopped flat-leaf (Italian) parsley, plus
   extra to garnish

Method

With adult help: Add one tablespoon of salt to a large saucepan and fill it three-quarters of the way up with water you have boiled in a kettle. Heat the salted water over high heat until boiling, then, wearing oven mitts, add the macaroni. Cook uncovered, stirring occasionally with a long-handled wooden spoon, until al dente (cooked through but still firm), about 11 minutes. While the macaroni is cooking, make the sauce.

With adult help: In a medium saucepan, melt the butter over medium heat. Add the flour and whisk for 1 minute – this butter and flour mixture is called a 'roux'. Turn off the heat and very gradually add the milk to the roux, whisking very well to avoid lumps.

With adult help: Once combined, turn the heat back on to medium–high and whisk the sauce until it bubbles and thickens, roughly 3–4 minutes. Reduce heat to low and add the cheese, nutmeg, pepper, paprika, salt and parsley. Stir until the cheese has melted and the sauce is smooth. Switch off the heat.

With adult help: Wearing oven mitts, pour the cooked macaroni into a colander positioned in the sink and drain well. Add the macaroni to the saucepan with the cheese sauce and stir the macaroni until it is well coated with cheese sauce. Spoon into bowls, sprinkle with extra parsley and enjoy immediately.

Equipment:

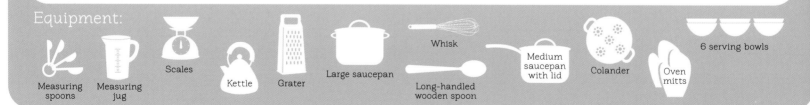

Measuring spoons · Measuring jug · Scales · Kettle · Grater · Large saucepan · Long-handled wooden spoon · Whisk · Medium saucepan with lid · Colander · Oven mitts · 6 serving bowls

Time-saving tips

Have all your equipment and ingredients ready

Find a kitchen hand to help you prepare the
ingredients ahead of time

Boil and salt your pasta water while you prepare
your ingredients

Use pre-grated cheese

Burritos

Burritos were a real favourite of mine when I was growing up. Healthy *and* delicious ... what more could you want?

Makes 4 large burritos
Prep time: 30 minutes
Cooking time: 30 minutes +

Ingredients

4 large flour tortillas

Spice mix

2 pinches hot paprika

½ teaspoon sweet paprika

½ teaspoon ground cumin

1 teaspoon onion powder

1 teaspoon garlic powder

2 pinches ground cinnamon

2 pinches ground cloves

1 teaspoon sea salt

2 pinches white pepper

1 tablespoon rice flour

Filling

2 tablespoons olive oil

1 small onion, sliced finely

250 g (9 oz) chicken breast fillets, cut into 1 cm (½ inch) cubes

200 ml (7 fl oz) water

50 g (1¾ oz/¼ cup) corn kernels (fresh or canned)

20 g (¾ oz/½ cup) finely shredded lettuce

1 medium tomato, cut into 1 cm (½ inch) cubes

Method

Pre-heat your oven to 200°C (395°F). Lay out 2 tortillas on each baking tray and set aside. Combine spice mix ingredients in a small bowl and set aside.

With adult help: Heat the olive oil in a frying pan over medium heat. Add the onion and cook, stirring regularly, for 5 minutes, or until softened and golden. Add the chicken and cook for 5 minutes. Keep stirring so all of the chicken cooks evenly. Once ready, remove from the heat and set aside.

With adult help: Heat a second frying pan over high heat and add the spice mix. Gradually whisk in the water, until well combined. Cook, stirring regularly, for around 2 minutes, or until thick. Reduce the heat to medium and add the chicken and corn to the spice mixture. Keep stirring to prevent sticking. Allow the chicken to heat for 5 minutes, or until cooked through. Remove from heat and set aside.

With adult help: Wearing oven mitts, place the baking trays in the oven on the middle and lower shelves. Heat the tortillas for about 3 minutes, or until just warmed through – they should not get crispy. Remove from the oven once ready.

Using tongs, arrange an even amount of lettuce and tomato down the centre of each tortilla. Spoon even amounts of the chicken filling on top to cover the salad. Carefully and tightly roll up each burrito so it resembles a fat sausage. If you're having trouble, ask an adult to help you with this!

If needed, place 2 toothpicks in each burrito to hold everything together. Serve immediately.

Equipment: Measuring spoons, Measuring jug, Chopping board, Sharp knife, Scales, 2 medium frying pans, Small bowl, Kitchen spoon, Whisk, Tongs, 2 baking trays, Toothpicks, Oven mitts

Time-saving tips

Have all your equipment and ingredients ready

Find a kitchen hand to help you prepare the ingredients ahead of time

Pre-heat your oven to 200ºC (395ºF) at least 20 minutes before cooking

Have oven trays positioned in the middle and lower shelves of the oven

Mexican chicken soup

One day I wanted to jazz up some chicken soup I made – and this Mexican-inspired dish was born!

Serves 5

Prep time: 20-30 minutes

Cooking time: 30 minutes +

Ingredients

2 tablespoons olive oil

1 small onion, quartered

2 garlic cloves, halved

1.5 litres (51 fl oz/6 cups) chicken stock
  (see Note)

½ teaspoon salt

2 spring onions (scallions)

4 chives

½ roast chicken breast fillet,
  finely shredded

1 tablespoon fresh coriander (cilantro)
  leaves, to garnish

50 g (1¾ oz) corn (tortilla) chips, to serve

Method

With adult help: In a large saucepan, heat olive oil over medium heat. Fry the onion and garlic until medium golden brown, about 5 minutes, stirring regularly with a wooden spoon. Once the onion and garlic are ready, carefully pour in the stock, then add the salt. Using scissors, very finely snip the spring onions and chives into the saucepan. Simmer the soup uncovered for roughly 20 minutes.

In the meantime, evenly divide the shredded chicken between each bowl.

With adult help: Wearing oven mitts, carefully ladle the soup into the bowls, discarding the onion and garlic. Sprinkle over the coriander leaves and serve immediately with a bowl of corn chips. Invite your dining companions to dip the chips into their soup as they tuck in!

Note

If using stock cubes, I recommend using 2½ cubes in 1.5 litres (51 fl oz/6 cups) of water.

Time-saving tips

Have all your equipment and ingredients ready

Find a kitchen hand to help you prepare the ingredients ahead of time

Make stock ahead of time or use quality ready-made chicken stock

Equipment:

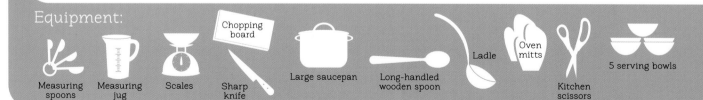

Measuring spoons | Measuring jug | Scales | Chopping board | Sharp knife | Large saucepan | Long-handled wooden spoon | Ladle | Oven mitts | Kitchen scissors | 5 serving bowls

chives and coriander

shredded chicken

corn chips

Spaghetti carbonara

Most people don't realise that authentic Italian carbonara recipes don't use cream. Golden, runny egg yolks are what make this dish creamy and luscious.

Serves 2 hungry people

Prep time: 30 minutes +

Cooking time: 30 minutes +

Ingredients

1 tablespoon salt, to add to pasta water
200 g (7 oz) spaghetti, snapped in half
2 tablespoons olive oil
1 small onion, finely diced
1 large garlic clove, finely grated or
  crushed
100 g (3½ oz) short-cut (back or
  Canadian) bacon, cut into 2 cm (¾ in)
  squares
80 g (2¾ oz) parmesan cheese, grated
½ teaspoon sea salt
3 pinches finely ground black pepper
2 egg yolks, whisked
Flat-leaf (Italian) parsley, to garnish
  (optional)

Method

With adult help: Add one tablespoon of salt to a large saucepan and fill it three-quarters of the way up with water you have boiled in a kettle. Heat the salted water over high heat until boiling, then, wearing oven mitts, carefully add the spaghetti. Stir regularly with a long-handled wooden spoon to prevent the pasta sticking. Cook for roughly 12 minutes, or until al dente (cooked through but still firm).

With adult help: While the pasta cooks, heat 1 tablespoon of olive oil in a large, deep frying pan over medium heat. Fry the onion and garlic until lightly golden, about 3 minutes, stirring regularly. Switch off the heat and transfer the onion and garlic to a small bowl.

With adult help: Heat the remaining tablespoon of olive oil in the same frying pan over medium heat. Fry the bacon pieces for 2–3 minutes, or until lightly golden. Turn off the heat and set the frying pan aside.

In a medium mixing bowl, combine the cheese, salt, pepper, bacon, onion and garlic, and set aside.

With adult help: Wearing oven mitts, carefully remove 60 ml (2 fl oz/¼ cup) of pasta water from the saucepan and set aside, then pour the cooked spaghetti into a colander positioned in the sink and drain. Return the spaghetti to the saucepan.

Pour the cheese mixture and egg yolks over the hot spaghetti, along with the reserved pasta water – this starchy water will help thicken and cook the sauce. Combine well. The heat from the pasta will cook the egg and melt the cheese. Serve immediately, garnished with parsley.

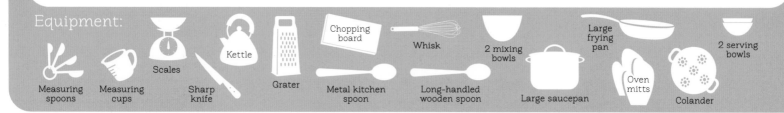

Equipment:
Measuring spoons · Measuring cups · Scales · Kettle · Sharp knife · Grater · Chopping board · Whisk · Metal kitchen spoon · Long-handled wooden spoon · 2 mixing bowls · Large saucepan · Large frying pan · Oven mitts · Colander · 2 serving bowls

Time-saving tips

Have all your equipment and ingredients ready

Find a kitchen hand to help you prepare the
ingredients ahead of time

Boil and salt your pasta water while you prepare
your ingredients

Tomato and risoni bake

Risoni is a small, rice-shaped pasta that is commonly used in Italian soups. Because of its shape, it's also known as 'orzo' which means 'barley' in Italian.

Serves 6

Prep time: 20 minutes

Cooking time: 30 minutes +

Ingredients

1 tablespoon sea salt, to add to pasta water
350 g (13½ oz) risoni
2 tablespoons olive oil
1 medium onion, finely diced
2 large garlic cloves, finely grated or
   crushed
2 small zucchini (courgettes), grated
15 g (½ oz/¼ cup) finely chopped chives
500 ml (17 fl oz/2 cups) tomato passata
   (puréed tomatoes)
1 teaspoon lemon juice
1 tablespoon sea salt
2 pinches finely ground black pepper
100 g (3½ oz) parmesan cheese, grated
2 teaspoons finely chopped flat-leaf
   (Italian) parsley leaves

Method

Pre-heat your oven to 240ºC (465ºF).

With adult help: Add one tablespoon of salt to a large saucepan and fill it three-quarters of the way up with water you have boiled in a kettle. Heat the salted water over high heat until boiling, then, wearing oven mitts, carefully add the risoni. Cook for 6 minutes, stirring regularly with a long-handled wooden spoon to stop the pasta sticking. Wearing oven mitts, pour the risoni into a colander positioned in the sink.

With adult help: In a medium saucepan, heat the oil over medium heat. Fry the onion, garlic and zucchini, stirring well with a wooden spoon until lightly golden, about 7 minutes. Add the chives, tomato passata, lemon juice, salt and pepper, and combine well. Stir the partially-cooked risoni through the sauce and cook, uncovered and stirring constantly, for 2 minutes. Switch off the heat.

Spoon the pasta mixture into a 20 cm x 30 cm (8 in x 12 in) baking dish. Sprinkle with the parmesan cheese, followed by the parsley.

With adult help: Wearing oven mitts, place the baking dish on the top shelf of your oven and bake for 10 minutes, or until the cheese is golden. Once again wearing oven mitts, remove the baking dish from the oven.

With adult help: Using a sharp knife, cut the pasta bake into 6 portions, being careful of any hot steam that might come out. Transfer to plates with a spatula and eat immediately.

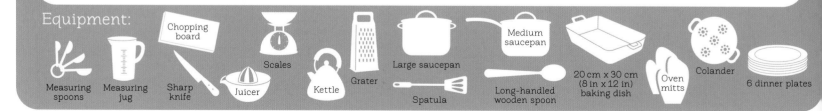

Equipment: Measuring spoons, Measuring jug, Chopping board, Sharp knife, Juicer, Scales, Kettle, Grater, Large saucepan, Spatula, Medium saucepan, Long-handled wooden spoon, 20 cm x 30 cm (8 in x 12 in) baking dish, Oven mitts, Colander, 6 dinner plates

Time-saving tips

Have all your equipment and ingredients ready

Find a kitchen hand to help you prepare the ingredients ahead of time

Pre-heat your oven to 240°C (465°F) at least 20 minutes before cooking

Have an oven tray positioned in the top shelf of the oven

Boil and salt your pasta water while you prepare your ingredients

Acknowledgements

Let's give it up for...

Anthony, my husband, for his love and support. A man of sound advice and bred from good stock.

My mum, Maria, who is still whipping up tasty treats today. I'm so lucky to have learnt from such an exceptional cook. Thanks for helping me in so many areas of my life.

My dad, Claude, whose advice and support I could not go without. His level-headedness is a perfect balance to my impulsive, creative and zany streak!

My two nonnas, Carmela and Lilliana, who I'm fairly sure never learnt from cookbooks, but are nonetheless a formidable force in the kitchen.

My brother and sister, J-Man (James) and Missy (Mia). Funny, smart and talented. They make my world a better place.

My multi-talented and beautiful friend Lisa Luscombe for helping me on the photoshoot.

The amazing little chefs, aged between 4 and 12, who were my recipe testers:

Livia and Emmy O'Dea, with mum Kelly; Meagan Hynson with aunty Michelle; Tanayah Godley with mum Natalie; Brianna and Charlize Birthsiel-Mulready with mum Kylie; Matthew and Allanah Glatzel with mum Karen; Lili Higham with mum Paige; Fintan and Cormac Hayes with mum Suzanne; Maggie and Spencer Park with mum Bev; Mariam Ashraf with mum Stephanie; Kiara Nici with mum Nicoletta; Lily Hill-Brooks and friend Shakira Meah with Lily's mum Nicky; Chloe Thicker with mum Kate; Toby Lott with mum Danielle; Lani Heyward with mum Polly; Katelyn Roddam with mum Mel; and Kyla del Castillo with mum Liezl.

The kind folks working at and for Hardie Grant Publishing for their support and for making my foodie dreams come true! In particular, heartfelt thanks to publishing director Paul McNally, photographer Mark Roper, home economist Caroline Jones, designers Simone Dutton and Megan Ellis, design manager Heather Menzies, managing editor Lucy Heaver and editor Rihana Ries.

And last but not least, a big thank you to Little Kitchen's customers. It's because of you that I get to do the work I love. Thanks for understanding how important it is to teach children how to cook.

Sabrina Parrini started cooking at a very young age, and food has always been a large part of her life.

Ever since watching her mother and grandmothers cook in their 'daggy' brown-tiled kitchen, she has been keen to share her enthusiasm for all things tasty and nutritious.

With a background in early childhood teaching and a love for food that doesn't come wrapped in plastic, Sabrina is one of Australia's foremost children's cookery experts. She opened Australia's first organic cookery school for children and runs kids' cookery lessons at major food festivals.

Sabrina has appeared and cooked on television, and regularly presents on Channel Nine's *Kitchen Whiz*. She has also penned two other cookbooks – *Little Kitchen* and *Little Kitchen: Around the World* – as well as a recipe journal for children.

Her Little Kitchen brand designs, manufactures and sources colourful cooking equipment made specifically for little hands and is the largest online retailer of children's cookware in Australia.

Find out more about Sabrina and Little Kitchen at www.littlekitchen.com.au.